DISCLAIMER: Romance, Power, & Religion in the Mind of a Godly Woman is a work of poetry. This statement is included to inform that the content may contain subjects that should be considered for mature readers only.

ROMANCE, POWER & RELIGION IN THE MIND OF A GODLY WOMAN

Lula Ellis

Romance, Power, & Religion in the Mind of a Godly Woman
By Lula Ellis

Cover Created by Jazzy Kitty Publications
Logo Designs by Andre M. Saunders/Jess Zimmerman
Editor: Anelda Attaway

© 2020 Lula Ellis
ISBN 978-1-7357874-8-0
Library of Congress Control Number: 2020924812

All rights reserved. This book is protected by the copyright laws of the United States of America. This book may not be copied or reprinted for commercial gain or profit. The use of short quotations or occasional page copying for personal or group study is permitted and encouraged. Permission will be granted upon request. For Worldwide Distribution. Printed in the United States of America. Published by Jazzy Kitty Publishing utilizing Microsoft Publishing Software and Bookcover Pro. Scriptures taken from the NKJV of the Bible and definitions from the Webster Dictionary.

Family First

The two most precious jewels are these two. My son Ishmael was the first and he was so sweet. I can remember being at the hospital and my sister coming into the room, thinking he was a White boy. He has the mind to be a millionaire and one day will become just that. His eyes are what captures the ladies' attention, and he says they get him what he wants.

My daughter which is a duplicate of me, and you can see she is so smart with the way she thinks and will one day be a doctor, I think. I welcome them to be a part of this book.

DEDICATIONS

This book is dedicated first to God who is head of my life.

Thank you for connecting me with Michael Guinn which is one that pushed me to be better and because of his passion has motivated me to write this first book.

Thank you for Ishmael and Chrysantheum for making me a mother that led by example.

Thank you for my sister Patricia Young & brother Curtis Young for helping me through life.

Thank you for my brother Leroy Carr & his wife Barbara Carr for the genuine love while in TX.

Thanks for my cousin Sharon Pilcher for being one of my biggest supporters.

Thanks to all my friends & families for tolerating me for this long.

TABLE OF CONTENTS

Introduction..i
Dear Diary..01
I Know Who I Am..04
You..07
I Got to Wait..08
This Battle is Not About You Boo..................................10
Dream Killers..12
Where is My Piece?..17
This is a Place that Come and Go................................20
The Story Doesn't End There.......................................23
Treasure Pain..26
This is Poetry...29
You Got Me Trapped..35
The Freedom of Peace..41
I Wish You'd Let Me Love You.....................................43
Hood Can Be Good..45
You My..49
Found Love Again..50
Just a Little Talk with Jesus...53
My Pride and Joy...55
Lady in Pink..57

TABLE OF CONTENTS

I'll Do Anything for You 59
I Was Made to Bend Not Break.. 60
I Got a Secret... 63
Lockdown for the Nation 65
Lifestyle Change 68
Things Got Real 70
Make God the First of All You Do 73
You Were Beautifully and Wonderfully Made by God............... 76
This Thing Called Women.. 78
Knock Out..83
Wake Up! Rise Up... 87
Ladies!...93
Have You Ever Been in a Place?...95
Corona!..98
Growing Up in the Mississippi Delta..102
Black Lady...106
College Student Essential Worker..108
Your Words Are Not the Truth...110
Black Men..112
To Be Normal Again...115
Fire Purifies...117
My Black Skin...119

TABLE OF CONTENTS

Kings & Queens!..123

We Will Win..125

About the Author..128

INTRODUCTION

Dear God,

You are the One that made this day possible. Thank You for trusting me to put words together to make a book. You have made me a part of history because I'm the first author in my family.

God, I always wonder why You love me so much. God, please take full control of my story and make a melody with it.

I pray that those that read will be blessed with the thoughts in my head. I'm not perfect, but through You, all is well.

Thank You for making this book a bestseller.

DEAR DIARY

Have you ever just wanted to vent without being judged? Living in a false reality, like you cannot break any given moment of what is going on in your mind?

As I write in my book can remember thinking that the more, I give the more things will get better being this good girl trying to make everybody else happy when you go through things that make you cold everyone around you think it is because you are getting old if someone tell me one more time I quote, "Lula you are a Christian." I really want to say do not remind me that is the reason I am in the place I'm in now. I think what if I did not have a conscientious there will be a lot of folks mess up right now. My mouth will not be filtered, and you will hate my guts every time I speak. You will swear I was possessed with the devil which that is a good place to behave. You ever just got to a place where you were tired of being nice? Now take your best shot you about to see what I am really made of. Lula you are not supposed to say that

Lula do not have sex before marriage. Lula do not marry him because he is not equally yoked with you. All these rules you are telling me to do you got to follow the same rules too. Have you ever just wanted to vent without being judged? You get to a point in your life where living comes easy you do not care what people think. Your mind becomes clear no bull crap can come near me at a point with saying if I go to Hell for being myself deserve to go a God you have not seen you think you've heard your neighbor that you've seen, you hear them all the time you can't step to them to ask, "How you are doing today?" And you don't even know their name.

You serve a loving God you say love is an action according to the Webster Dictionary:

1. A strong feeling of affection and concern toward another person, as that arising from kinship or close friendship.

2. A strong feeling of affection and concern for another person accompanied by sexual attraction.

3. An intense emotional attachment to something, as

to a pet or treasured object.

You love your dog better than you love man. You make sure they eat, bathe, and potty; you always there to give them a helping hand.

Have you ever just wanted to vent without being judged? As I attempt to move forward with my day venting helps keep the doctor away. My physical help is extremely good; it's my mental dealing with things that don't have value in my life. It is trying to take me outtake time to let it all out. You will see how being free is what it's all about.

When I'm alone it is the best place for a memo. One to answer to no one to judge what I do. I make a lot of mistakes too; my mind plays tricks on me from day to day. If you want to be connected to me; do know that you can't be in bondage complaining about everything that is non-important to men. The Holy Spirit within will set you free.

Lula Ellis
I KNOW WHO I AM

It started when I was a little girl

I always wondered.

WHO AM I?

Even though I Lived in the Projects

My Mind was in the Palace

I'm not a Product of what I See

I was Created to be Royalty

I KNOW WHO I AM

My Walk, my Smile with a Dimple on the Sides

My Speech, My Reach, My Presence, My Style

When I Walk in the Room my Beauty Shows

NO NEED TO SAY

BECAUSE EVERYONE KNOWS

I KNOW WHO I AM

I was Created to Lead, NOT Follow

I'm Allergic to ANYTHING that's Hollow

You can't be part of My Amazing Space

If my Heart of Gold you CAN'T Embrace

I KNOW WHO I AM

Created to Blend in like a Chameleon

This Shade of Skin fits ANY Environment

My Surroundings DON'T make me

I make My Surroundings, you see

Because of the Life I've Lived

And it's MANY Test

Yes, I DEMAND the Respect that I get

You see,

I KNOW WHO I AM

Deep inside is the Strength of Me

My Soul, My Spirit, My Freedom is FREE

Always Carry yourself as you want to be Seen

Like Ladies of Royalty, you are Queens

So that everyone you Meet

Sees a Shining Star

Remember it all begins with

KNOWING WHO YOU ARE

YOU

That Day ALMOST Night!

You came without a Fight Unexpected

And wasn't Protected

Fallen to the Floor

Heart beating for more

I Rolled, I Rolled, I Cried, I Died

To everything that I once knew

YOU, YOU, YOU

Came into My Life to make me New

When I Woke Up it was YOU,

When I Laid Down it was YOU

When I Turned Around it was YOU

And I'm so Glad after that Long Process

THAT IT ENDED WITH YOU

I GOT TO WAIT

It's almost Here

And so very Near

I CAN FEEL IT!

I CAN TOUCH IT

Oh God!

When will that Day Be?

When my Husband is Close to Me?

I GOT TO WAIT

I Dream about Him

And Visualize that day will Soon Come

God you were the One that made me from his Rib

WHY I GOT TO WAIT

The Promise is so Close,

That he can be just My Dose of Everything

I've been Waiting for

I GOT TO WAIT

The Lord knows the Time and Hour
Of when it will be
All I want is for Him to Inform Me

IT'S GOOD TO WAIT
Because this will mostly be the Mate
That God made just for me
Can't wait until he gets on those Knees

This Day is ALMOST Here
And I tell you I can Hear
The Wedding Bells Ringing

And this Time it's True
Because God MADE Him for You
I THANK GOD I WAITED

THIS BATTLE IS NOT ABOUT YOU BOO

You Sit and you Think it's all about you
However, the devil is Plotting to Destroy
What's about to come True

THIS BATTLE IS NOT ABOUT YOU BOO!

You are a Woman of Gain
And a Woman of Pain
The devil knows the Plan for your Life
And most definitely don't want you to Rain

THIS BATTLE IS NOT ABOUT YOU BOO!

You don't know the Destiny you Carry
It's so Powerful and Contrary to all the Things
That happened to you

God is about to Shine

And make all your Dreams Come True

I know you thought this Battle was about you

With your Flip Flops and High Heels too

THIS BATTLE IS NOT ABOUT YOU BOO!

God Formed you from your Mother's Womb

To carry a Word that would Change a Nation

So, get off your Butt and Face

This Fight with Patience

God is about to take you to Heights

UNKNOWN TO MAN

So, DON'T Sweat the Small Things

DREAM KILLERS

As I Drive just Thinking about my Vibe

My Mind is Clear

Because I need to know what's out Here

ARE YOU A DREAM KILLER?

On the 4TH of July I just CAN'T stand by

The Weather is so Sweet I'm just ready to Meet

Some people who are Pushers, NOT Killers,

Feeling up the Moment with Fillers

And Even though this is a Day off

I can't Sit Still because they are out here

To reach beyond Stars

Just before the fireworks go off.

Tell me...ARE YOU A DREAM KILLER?

I need to know Before

I Open My Door

To all these Dreams Pouring from my Soul

A killer will Plot Out ways to Destroy

Not only your Dreams

But your Motivation to Win

SO, DON'T GIVE IN

Tell me where you are,

because I'm about to walk into my destiny

And I don't need you near

ARE YOU A DREAM KILLER?

ARE YOU OR YOU OR YOU?

Listen! "Hear Me Well!"

My Phrase when I Drop this Powerful Nugget

In your Ear

You got to be Very Attentive

I'll make myself Clear

You got to Silence the Noise

Because what I'm about to Say

Will change your Thinking in Many Ways

ARE YOU A DREAM KILLER?

As I look up the word KILLER in the Webster
"A PERSON OR THING THAT KILLS"
As simple as that so don't get caught up in Stacks

1 Tim 6:10
"FOR THE LOVE OF MONEY IS
THE ROOT OF ALL EVIL"

You got to be More Careful
Because ALL Money is NOT Good

The enemy tries to Lure you in
With what you Love the Most
Not knowing it can KILL YOUR DREAMS
And EVERYTHING you stand for

You got to do an Environment Check
To make sure the people are for you
And not for what you can do

ARE YOU A DREAM KILLER?

It's NOT too late to Change Your Mind
Don't Hate on the Rhymes on my Tongue
Just say OUCH and Move On

You don't EVER Support unless it's FREE
And you ONLY Show up
When you're up to Speak

Take the Time
To make Somebody Else's Day
Because when you do
God will make a Way Just for You
And also make your DREAMS COME TRUE

Don't be the one that's Hating in Silence
You can do what you want to do too
I'm so Glad we all were Created for a Purpose
And your DREAMS Matter Too

I'm Hopeless WITHOUT you
So, no one can Kill what God made to Live
JUST KNOW WHO YOU ARE
AND CONTINUE TO DREAM!

WHERE IS MY PIECE?

My Life is like a PUZZLE

Because it starts off All Over the Place

Don't make it Complicated

It's Right in your Face

When you think the PIECES fit

You will have to Rearrange again

One thing I do know is that

The PIECES make a Whole

And the Story of My Life hasn't been Told

WHERE IS MY PIECE

When I Realize that I am NOT my own

I make EVERY Moment Count

Until God takes me Home

I was thinking that

If I'm going to make these PIECES fit

I got to have a Vision

What are you Seeing Life to be

God has Given you all the Tools

Please ask Him to Help you see

Where is My PIECE

You only have one Life to Live

Don't be Afraid to Give

You Deserve the Whole that this PUZZLE will make

Don't allow ANYONE to Continue to take what

You have to Remember

All the PIECES are here in this Room

Take a Look Around

You have all Types of People around you

They are the Ones that can Help you Through

We need the Difference that each other Brings
The PIECE OF MY PUZZLE is in your Hands
God knew EXACTLY what He was Doing

When He made me Darker than you
Just keep on Believing
AND THE PICTURE IN THE PUZZLE
WILL COME TRUE

THIS IS A PLACE THAT COME AND GO

I'm sitting wondering how did I get back here? My mind is exhausted, and my body is confused. I can remember the day I met him. We were in the park and he was teaching me some protection moves

I thought to myself, *"look at those arms and those moves with his hands."*

He was of a different belief, but I didn't care. He came to one of my events to perform; I can do this all day long. I can remember being invited to this beautiful house with four rooms two baths. The carpet was so clean and the furniture so fancy.

He took me upstairs and asked me to help him hang clothes. We talked and talked for so long; then he began to touch my hair. I couldn't help but stair at the chocolate covered arms. This man was such a charm.

I was very vulnerable and was dealing with loneliness too. He laid me on the bed and opened up my legs. My body was saying yes, but my heart knew it's not the best thing to do.

He moved my panties to the side, and he went in and out. He was done in no time and at that moment, I began to cry. Why did I allow him in my soul? I knew that soul tie would take control. I started crying and running out the room. He caught me in his arms to ask me what was wrong I told him I wasn't ready for this.

He looked me in my eyes to tell me, *"I won't hurt you I promise."* But his words turned to dust.

He asked my hand in marriage. We went to buy the ring, and this was the happiest time I've had in a long time.

We were not married a year until he began to act funny. I remember him in the kitchen while we had visitors. He looked so mad as I was telling them how wonderful he was. He walked out of the room only to tell me later he wanted a divorce. My heart dropped to the floor and I couldn't breathe. I waited 12 years to find love again only for it to leave. It's funny how you can be happy one day and depressed the next. This placed a big scar in my heart; I blamed God for not protecting me but only if I could hear God tell me Lula! *"He's not the one, if you stay with him, he will break your heart."* This taught me a lesson to wait and pray it though.

When I found love after this it was in God; even though I was in church all my life. When you realize how much love God has inside of you God won't put no more on us than we can bear.

This situation made me aware of the people around me and to be careful too. Your trials come to make you stronger, wiser, and better. Don't regret it but celebrate!

THE STORY DOESN'T END THERE

It started at the age of 3, the biggest house in the middle of nowhere began to fall before my mother's eyes. I was asleep on the sofa not knowing that I was faced with death only to awaken to flames and a light that led me out of the building. This was a faith move not knowing that the light led me out to my family.

As I ran to my mother the house falls down behind me. My mother grabbed me in despair. The story doesn't end there.

At the age of 9 here we go again in the hospital watching the nurses run in with two equipment's in their hands. They placed one on the right and one on the left as they put me out of the room. Then mother was in a fight only to have them come to the waiting room 15 minutes later to say that she didn't make it.

As everyone grabbed each other with tears down their face, "She's gone," they said. However, the nightmare didn't end there.

The only person that was close to mom was shot

"Pow, Pow, Pow" about 10 times in front of the me and her two boys. She's gone as the gunman turned around with the gun pointed at me as I was curved up on my bedroom floor.

"Come go with me," he said with the gun pointed to my head.

He put me in the truck as he drove away. He went to a barn to hide his SUV truck in a full of hay.

I began to think, *"Will this nightmare end?"*

As I sat in the SUV covered in hay only to hear the gunman say, "I should have had you instead of your auntie," as I put my pants back on not remembering all that's going on.

What is it for me to do as I fall asleep only to awake to reality as we wait again until night passed.

In my mind I thought, *"When will this stop? When will the nightmare end?"* I can remember the day he was on a pay phone.

Can you imagine this all day long? His father, a cop convinced him to let me go and turn himself in. He obeyed and I was back with my family again.

I want to let someone know today! The storm don't last always because it just ended!

TREASURED PAIN

It's a Tragedy to have a GREAT TREASURE wrapped in so much Hurt and Pain. I choke to death on my Tears because I have the ability to make the world go around, but my Past keeps trying to take over my Future. I can't have a good Conversation without thinking someone is out to get me.

My Relationships ONLY lasting a Year
Can't Hug my son and daughter
Can't say Good Morning

And I'm always wondering who's going to leave next. My Past keeps Ruining my Happiness because I just sit and think what it would be like if I only had a Mother & Father.

I can Imagine my dad would have been very Protective and my mother very Lovable.
How can I Teach my Own when I was left Alone?
I accept the Distinction of others because that's what

I'm familiar with. Now, don't get me wrong, my life is still Good. But what happened to my Childhood I can imagine Running from my Past. But every time I start, the Finish Line still seems so Far.

No matter How Much I Pray
I just can't get away from a Place that will always Stay
Because it Made me who I am Today

And I'm Sad because my Past just won't leave me alone. If I had Power of my Tongue like the Bible say, I would Command the Past to leave me Alone and Never Return.

I will not be your Prisoner ever again
I'm more than a Conqueror
I shall Live and not Die
I'm Victorious and Unstoppable

HOW YOU LIKE ME NOW?

This Power is so Strong

I can just go On and On

My Past is NO LONGER a Threat

I now Know where my Power is

What my Power is

That I am Powerful

Always Watch what you Say

Cause the Power is in my Tongue

So Past, POOF Be Gone!

THIS IS POETRY

THIS IS THE POETRY I WRITE

Sitting in my Bed at 4:46 am

Crying Tears of Sorrow

Not knowing where to Begin

My Heart is so Heavy

Seem like Everything around is so Still

The World is so Corrupted

And it seems like Nobody Cares

I don't want to Post ANOTHER Post

Or Pray ANOTHER Prayer

I'm just Lying here Wondering

Does Anybody Care

Oh! I don't want to go to Work today

This is one of those Moments that

I just don't care

These days Come and Go

Nobody knows how this Spirit Attacks me

In the Mid-Night Hour

I tried to find Medicine,

But I was out this day

All I want is for my Brain to Stay Happy

Not think of Bad Thoughts

It's a Constant Fight because I don't want to give up

Have you ever felt like you were in a Planet of your own?

Who can hear me?

Oh, I'm so alone

Why can't Good Things Happen

Every minute of the day

This Spirit is trying to Take Over

But my Heart is Fighting to get away

I'm Exhausted from Thinking about

What it's Doing to me

I can't have a Good Relationship

Because I'm trying to Break Free

From a Spirit that Married Me

I don't remember saying, "I Do."

I feel so Hopeless at this Moment

I don't know what to do

My Heart is so Heavy

And my Mind is too

I want a Divorce from you Spirit.

Oh! That's No Problem

Seems that they all Leave Away

I'm Ready for that Day

To Marry someone that Will Take Me

And my Problems too

Don't Leave me EVER again

And NO MATTER what will stay

What's wrong with a woman wanting to be Captured

And Protected

By someone that REALLY CARES

No Matter What

No Friend to Call and No Family to See

My Heart is so Heavy,

I wish this Spirit will let me be

On this day

I wish Raindrops will Fall

My Mind is NOT Clear, and I don't see it all

I got an Hour before my Day Starts again

This Spirit is So Strong,

It's getting in my hand

Where did these Insecurities come from
And will I EVER be Free?
I'm not Jealous of Anyone
It's just something going on Inside of Me

Can ANYBODY Hear me?
And Can You Help?

I can't Stop Crying
My Stomach is so Tight
I got ONE more Hour to Sleep tonight

One day I will be Free, I thought
This Day will come so Peaceful I will be
This World is so Corrupted alone with me

Life knows how to Knock You Down
At the Wrong Time
Who wants to Love Someone that's
So, Broken Sometimes

I wonder God, where are you?

This thing called Life is so Hard and Cruel

I can just see Freedom from this Body made of Dirt

My Spirit wants it and Can't Wait

Don't let the Spirit of Depression

Get you Alone

Because it will Marry you

And take you Home

When that Spirit comes

Know that someone Loves you

MORE THAN YOU

YOU GOT ME TRAPPED

This is a Conversation
I'm having with my Heart

What do you mean you In Love Again?
I'm Minding my own Business with my Destiny
In God's Hands

Why DIDN'T you Ask me First?
Before you Chose this Man?
You ALWAYS Getting me in Trouble
Only to Break Again

You DON'T Understand
But you think He's the One
When the Radio Plays our Favorite Song

What do mean and what do you do?
When the Man that you Fight
Is the One that Got you?

He calls me Babe and Sweetie too

You ALWAYS Fall for him

When he comes Next to you

YOU GOT ME TRAPPED

Once again, I got to Test him out

By Showing him how

I can Open My Mouth

My Heart always want to Love

The very Opposite

Heart stop Moving and going Forward

Without my Permission

You got me up all times of the Night

On a Mission

If I could control my destiny with him,

We will be like Romeo and Juliet

You ain't going nowhere unless it's death

YOU GOT ME TRAPPED

As I Rub your Chest

My Poor Heart is a Mess

When are you going to Stop letting your Heart

Push you Around

To find out Later it Let you Down

At One Point I thought

I could Control who my Heart Loves

That was a Joke, and my Life moves Forward

Okay Heart, wait just one minute

My thoughts are not Clear

You just Beat Out of Control

When he's Near

He makes me do some Crazy Stuff

Like make a Dance Video at the Movies

Of My Butt

Chase him around the Table
Until I'm Tired
Spend all my Money on Things
That doesn't matter

I'm just a Puppet you see
My Heart just makes a Fool out me

He makes me want to FaceTime him
Every chance I get
Only to Continue asking him
Where you at?

When he Touches me, the World Stops
It starts Back up
When he's on Top of the mountain
For those that think He's on Top of me
I got to be Very Clear you see

To all of you that Thought

You were In Love

You got to tell your Heart what to do

Before it makes a Mockery out of you

YOU GOT ME TRAPPED

I'm so Stuck like Crazy Glue

I'm so Helpless without you

What a great Choice you made so Far

This Last Man Just Stole my Heart

It's okay when the Feelings are Mutual

HE'S TRAPPED TOO AND UNSTOPPABLE

If you make God, the Center of the two

He will make your Dreams Come True

Falling in Love is EASY to do

When the other person Feels the Same Way too

It makes things Easier

You see

And I don't mind him being

TRAPPED BY ME

THE FREEDOM OF PEACE

There is No Hindrance or Restraints

From the Peace that BELONGS to you

This World makes you Choose

Between the two

Why can't you have One WITHOUT the Other?

Because it Goes Against EVERYTHING Taught

It's said that there's

NO FREEDOM WITHOUT PEACE

Not knowing that there's a Difference in Mind

You can have FREEDOM BUT NO PEACE

A Door can be Opened BUT a Closed Mind

Won't allow you to see

That you have the PEACE to Walk Freely

Knowing that on the Other Side

Is the PEACE you Need

FREEDOM doesn't just come

Because someone says

Nor a Letter of Declaration stating you're Free

That Freedom comes from knowing who you are

Your Place in the World,

Your Heart and Path

YOUR FREEDOM IS YOUR PEACE

Because NOTHING can Stop

What was ALWAYS meant to be

I WISH YOU'D LET ME LOVE YOU

I WISH YOU WOULD LET ME LOVE YOU

I Try, I Try & I Try to be that Person that can be
The Harmony in your Mind and your Dreams

I WISH YOU WOULD LET ME LOVE YOU

I'm the one that will Run your Bath
Make your Breakfast in Bed
Rub your Feet and Head

I WISH YOU WOULD LET ME LOVE YOU

My Love for you is Blind
My Heart for you will Unwind
I can't Breathe without your Presence
I want to make you mine Forever

I WISH YOU WILL LET ME LOVE YOU

You're the Apple of my Eyes
Without you I will Die

Like the Flowers WITHOUT Water
So, STOP Running from the Truth
I'm Hopeless without you

I WISH YOU WILL LET ME LOVE YOU

I will Kiss you on your Head
Go Down around your Legs
To the Bottom of your Feet
Until our Bodies meet

We will become One in Spirit
That day will Come when you go Up and Down
As you Flip me Around and Go Downtown

I WISH YOU WOULD
LET ME LOVE YOU FOREVER

HOOD CAN BE GOOD

At work 6 am in the Morning

Me, Asian Dude, and two Young Ladies

That Stood Out the Most

They Talked so much

I thought they were a Host

Or something from a Tale

That Happened in the Hood

The Asian guy got close to my Desk

And Whispered in my Ear

He said, "Lula no offence, but you don't act like them."

I thought, *"What does he mean?"*

I don't act like them

Because they bring more attention

I could ever dream

He said, "Pay Attention when they Walk

And have a Translator when they Talk."

They Walked to their Desk

They both had on a Similar Dress

It was Pink with Black Tights

I thought to myself, *"Where they are going tonight?"*

When they started Talking the Story Began

The story from the Tales in the Hood

They both were Friendly and that was Good

The Ladies started Looking up and down

Snapping their Fingers and Throwing their Hair

It took all of me NOT to Stare

But when they started talking this is what they said

"Where they do that at boo?"

"Who they think them talking too?"

I turned around and Looked at my Co-worker

This is what he was Talking about

I Swear I thought we were in a Club

And who would have Guess

What was in their Mugs

This was a Story of Tales

FROM THE HOOD

Even through the Ladies were Good

YOU MY

YOU MY

You My Cream in my Coffee

You My Sugar in my Tea

You My Hands to Massage my Back

My Cover all over me

You My Flour to make my Cake

You my Oven when I'm ready to Bake

My Back Pockets on my Pants

My Lotion on my Hands

You My Mind when I'm Ready to Think

My Soap when I Stink

My Shower when I need a Bath

My Calculator when I do my Math

You My Socks on my Feet

My Husband when we Meet

YOU MY EVERYTHING

And that's Everything to me

FOUND LOVE AGAIN

Where did it go?!

Sitting in my chair with my feet up thinking,

"What happened and how can I get it back?"

Can't breathe from crying Tears of Pain

And Joy in the same Tear

Who wants it when every time your Smile

Turns to Sorrow?

I said to God,

"Please take me away because every minute of Pleasure

Soon turns to Pain."

How can you?

A loving God creates people

That have so much Evil in their Heart

That they Breathe to Kill every Happy Soul

Because they don't want to Live

Where did it go?

I can See it and Image it

But I can't Touch it

I thought, *"Does it really exist?"*

I started after it again

I fell Flat on my Face

Only to Numb away from something that truly Exist

But how can I Obtain it and Multiply it?

Until one day

I heard a voice from Heaven say,

"It's in Me remember the One that Wiped your Tears

And took away all Fears

You Remember…

The One that made a way out of no way

The one that Turned Water to Wine

The one that Created your Mind

I'm the One you're looking for

I'm the One that will open the door

To everything you ask Me to do

All you have to do is Believe

JUST A LITTLE TALK WITH JESUS

When I'm Alone in my Room

I Stare at the Walls

Just waiting for a voice from Heaven to Call

Little Child, Little Child

If I did it before I can do it again

JUST A LITTLE TALK WITH JESUS

THAT'S ALL I NEED

Just want Him to Hold me and Touch me

That would make it Alright

That Gentle Whisper in the Night

JUST A LITTLE TALK WITH JESUS

THAT'S ALL I NEED

MY PRIDE MY JOY NEED I SAY MORE?

MY PRIDE MY JOY

MY PRIDE MY JOY Need I say more

My Ish, My Chrys they can't be missed

One Boy One Girl

They Changed my World

One in the Hotel

And One on the Beach

Who would have thought?

Our Paths would Reach

A Point of No Return

Even if we Tried

God gave you a Part of my Heart

And that we CANNOT Hide

LADY IN PINK

LADY IN PINK

MISS AKA PRETTY LADY IN PINK
But he didn't know I was a Freak
In my Mind, Oh let me see
Let's go Down Memory Lane
And I'll let you Decide for me

January 1st was that Big Day
Man! So happy and Carefree

I'm in the back Putting on my Makeup
And my Hair was so Sweet that Long Pretty Dress
Man, it Compliments me

We waited a year before he tasted the sweet melody
Between my Legs or my Thighs

I thought to myself,
"He's hypnotized not seeing the baggage on the inside of me
Just one cut and he will see the outer appearance
is not what it's cracked up to be."

PRETTY LADY IN PINK

But rooting to the Core

He'll be alright, I thought
But oh, there's much more
He didn't know he Married a Whore

Not what you think
But a Prostitute to all the things
That were giving me a Fix

A cheap thrill that lasts a minute
only to realize I'm still in it

The moral of this story is…
don't judge a book by its cover
The lady in pink might not be that sweet

I'LL DO ANYTHING FOR YOU

This is the way to make a person you Love Feel Good

I'll Pay Bills for you

I'll go up and down a hill for you

I'LL DO ANYTHING FOR YOU

I'll make a Meal for you, Be Still for you

I'LL DO ANYTHING FOR YOU

I'll get on Both Knees for you

Just to Cough and Breathe for you

I'LL DO ANYTHING FOR YOU

I'll Turn you Over and Rub your Tummy

I'll feed you Honey

I'LL DO ANYTHING FOR YOU

Laila a girl's Best Friend

I WAS MADE TO BEND NOT BREAK

You don't know me

And you sure didn't form me!

I was created by God

To take a Lickin' and keep Tickin'

I WAS MADE TO BEND BUT NOT BREAK

Like the Trees in the Miami wind

No matter how Hard they Bend

They were made to Bounce Back

I WAS MADE TO BEND BUT NOT BREAK

Disappointment didn't do it and Trials...

I got through it

You thought I wouldn't get through it

Depression would not let me be Great

But God said NOT SO Just Wait

"No weapon that's formed against me shall prosper"

I WAS MADE TO BEND NOT BREAK

So, Hold your Head up Lady
You got This and More
God created you to TAKE MORE than you Think
I WAS MADE TO BEND BUT NOT BREAK

I GOT A SECRET

I GOT A SECRET

One Hand over your Left eye

One Hand over the Right

Don't you Peek a Boo

Or you will Start a Fight

In my Mind and in my Dream

When you Step into the Room

You make me Scream

Holler, Holler Loud and Clear

I GOT A SECRET

That you MUST hear

He don't even know

He's my #1 Fan

I'll give him Two Weeks

And he'll be my Man

I GOT A SECRET

And I can't wait to Share

It's the one that told me

To Cut My Hair

It's either Holy Matrimony or Doom

It's going to be One or the Other

And guess what?

He's in this Room!

LOCKDOWN FOR THE NATION

News filled with Body Bags

Families not able to have

A Decent Burial

Unbelievable! What I'm thinking

Lying in my Bed with Tears in my Eyes

Looked up!

God what's happening?

My mind began to Wonder

As my Conversation with God got Real

Just imagine God talking back

Daughter you have the Chance to get it Right

Repent! Turn from your Wicked ways

Make Me the Center of your Life again

Fear became my Friend

Didn't know who to Trust
Listening to Everybody's Revelation

God was trying to tell me something
What was going on Inside of me Showed

Looking in the Mirror
Hate, Disappointment, Unforgiveness too
All became a Part of my Life

It's time to purge! Let is all go
Thoughts after each Cough
Corona got me Feeling Crazy up in here
Let me make sure Everything is Clear

Debt Paid in Full
Before this Virus kills me
Made a couple of Phone Calls
Moving through the week Preparing

Repent!

Turn from your Wicked Ways

God began to Speak Again

Forgive me for Sin has taken Control

Falling to my Knees

Please Spare me this Day

Oh Lord

Making it Right with God

Is what I'm Thinking

When Glorious that Day comes

God! Please say Well Done

LIFESTYLE CHANGE

MY LIFE CHANGED FOR THE BEST

More Trips to the Grocery Store

More Fruits and Vegetables in my Basket

No more eating Fast Food

No more Coffee in the Morning

No more Sweets at Night

MY LIFE CHANGED FOR THE BEST

Working from Home save me Gas

More Washing my Hands

Sanitizer in my Bag

MY LIFE CHANGED FOR THE BEST

More Walking the Dog

More Cleaning her Paws

More Attention she Gets

MY LIFE CHANGED FOR THE BEST

Closer Relationship with my Family
More Calls to be Call

More looking Forward to Live Videos
Just to Cheer someone Else on

More Money in my Pocket
Helps Pay ALL Bills on Time
Before all this happened
Couldn't keep a Dime

MY LIFE CHANGED FOR THE BEST

Better relationship with my Future Love
More time to Play Silly Games
More time to Invest in More
More time to think about the Next Move
More time to Appreciate Life

THINGS GOT REAL

My Best Friend in High School
NO ONE could Touch My Heart
THE WAY SHE DID

We had an Unusual Relationship
We both were Home Bodies
Didn't do much like Teens our age did

No Smoking, No Drinking, No Boys
Its funny people thought
We were a Couple

Our fun was Sitting at the House Telling Stories
Watching our Favorite Shows on TV

After High School went to College
We grew apart Unexpectedly
Last we Talked was Over Lunch

She began to tell me about her Little Boy
Reached in her Pocket gave me a Picture
Oh! How we Missed each other

We talked over the Phone for awhile
Not knowing One Day too soon
I'll be Saying my Last Goodbye

Got a call on April 20, 2020
The Coronavirus took My Friend away

This became More Real to me than ever
All Good Times
Rehearsing in my Mind

Begin to Wish we were Still Talking
Maybe my Prayer would've Saved her
Who was there when she said her Last Goodbye?

Things just Got Real
How did her Family Feel?
Why didn't someone Tell Me Sooner?
My friend was an Essential Worker

Such a Good Heart she had
God will be Please with her
My girl just had a Good Heart
No need to Mourn Forever

My friend is in a Better Place
Heaven just gained an Angel

Romance, Power, & Religion in the Mind of a Godly Woman

MAKE GOD THE FIRST OF ALL YOU DO

WHAT'S REALLY GOING ON

Is what I'm Thinking

God it got to be More to this than this

I'm so tired of Poems of Racism and Injustice

We don't even help each other without a Mess

We have more Black families Fighting and Dysfunctional

And think that's Blessed

What are we going to do about what's Left

Let's Show them how we can Walk together,

Talk together it's going to always be a Text

If you're telling me I can walk in a Library today

Read a Book without having to Sneak around

Before Master looks

On just yesterday I got to witness a Black man

From East Texas named Mike Guinn bring together

Whites, Blacks, Asians, Hispanic and more

To an MLK Writing Class

That's what I called a Movement

And that's what he was Created for

Only to Hear one of us say I got Strategies

I can use for my Workshop

That Statement alone makes me Question

The Motives of why we go to each other's Events

Are we there to Support and Push my Brother/Sister

I've seen so many Mothers Trusting men

With their daughter

Only to Find out later it's Disappointing

You've heard of all the Stories

These Little Ones don't even Deserve it

Who can tell me how to Help the Lost

And make the Great! Great?

My heart is so Heavy and Confused too
God, please tell me what to do
When another Little Person is Taken
What type of World are we Making?

We stand before You with all these Cliques
Behind Closed Doors we in a Maze
You Decide what your Purpose is Today

Always make God the First of all you do
He is the One to make the Dream Come True

YOU WERE BEAUTIFULLY AND WONDERFULLY MADE BY GOD

Nobody can Downgrade

What God Upgraded from your Mother's Womb

You're trying your Best to make everybody else Happy

But what are they doing for you?

You get Extra and you want a Share

They are only Concerned about what you do

They don't want to know what they can do for you

Don't allow your Success

Put you in a State of Mind

Nobody can help you

Because I've been doing this for Quite Some Time

The day you Feel you DON'T need Help

God will Allow something to Remind you of Yourself

You are that Diamond that has to have a Key to get too

Your those Clothes that have a Gray Barcode

You better not Walk out the Door

It will Explode

You're that Car that's on the Show Floor

Not the one in the Corner outside the Door

You're that Organic Food that's Expensive to Buy

You're that Job that requires more than One Interview

You're that Passenger that's Seated First Class

You're that one with the Wine Class

You're VIP status and won't Settle for Less

You're the one that don't have Time for Mess

Lula Ellis
THIS THING CALL WOMEN

Didn't know that being a Woman

Would make me Change each year

I turn Another Age

On my way to Mississippi

I stopped to get some Gas

And bought me an Ice Cream Bar

As I Drive my Brother's Wife Nephew back home

My Stomach started Cramping and Bubbling

I had to Squeeze my Butt so tight

To keep from Exploding

Had to get to Nearest Store

Need I say more

Only to find out at the age of 30

I was Lactose Intolerant

It's that time again when I turned 40
My Body started acting like
It had a Mind of its Own

Being that I'm a Church Girl
I can remember calling the Church Mothers over
Because I wanted a Fix
For my Unstoppable Sex Drive

Told the Church Mothers about
How I'm not Longing for someone
But something

The two Mothers Prayed like
I was Processed with Legions of Demons

They put Oil everywhere in the House and on Me
When they Left, I thought to myself,
"I'm not healed, I'm just an Oily Freak

My Body is still Longing for Affection

That's Normal when you've had it before

At this age call 40

My Tolerance is at 0 now

If my Son or Daughter were to say, but mom

I'll Choke them until their Voices Changed!

When Driving on the Highway

I feel like nobody should be on this Freeway, but me!

I say things like,

"Why are these folks not at home at this time?"

Like everybody on the Road should go Home

Until I reach my Destination!

My Food Choices is all over the Place

My Body Weight is Picking up Faster than before

And it's NOT going anywhere

Went into the store the other day

tried to buy pants I thought was my size

but not anymore

I've NEVER had a Problem with

The Clothes being Too Little

My size now is Unpredictable

I don't know what to get

I can remember Loving my High Heel Shoes

I'll wear them to Work even as a Cashier

Now my Outfit can be Cute

But those Shoes better be Comfortable

I remember going to the Doctor

Because I thought my Ankle was Sprung

It's not Sprung you just Getting Older

And the things that was No Problem

Has become one

I can't Stand, Walk, or Drive now for a period of time
Or my Ankles will look like I have Weights on them
This was one of the things I Couldn't Believe

One morning just Jumping Up
And tried to Spring out of Bed
My Mind was in the Bathroom
But my Body hit the floor. Unbelievable!

My legs didn't have any feelings to them
And it took a while before I could get up

My girl told Lula,
"You'll getting older you got to sit there for a minute
And then get up."

Ladies, take it One Day at a Time
And remember you're always Changing
So just go with the Flow

KNOCK OUT

Are you ready for the Fight of your Life?

With my Pretty Pink Lace

On my Chocolate Covered Face

With Heels high enough

They don't make them like this Anymore

You have the Choice to Walk away

You might Survive and your Fans might say

"Just choose Wisely before the Fight began."

One wrong Move,

You'll have Syrup all over your Hands

Close your Eyes

Let me take you for a Ride

To this Show Down in the Boxing Ring

It's either You or Me

Put this Oil all over the Lollipop in my hand

Don't Mess with me

I'm known for KNOCKING OUT my man

Put you to Sleep

You only get One Round

I'm known to KNOCK YOU OUT

With your Thumb in your Mouth

Don't Step in the Ring

Unless you're ready to Challenge my Fantasy

In this Corner you have the Number One

The only Champion of the Universe

Dimples is known for Deep

I mean Deep Pain that feels like Pleasure

Don't Step in the Ring

If you can't come Multiple Rounds

Dimples will ALWAYS take you Down

She's known to Get on Her Knees

With a Pop Sickle aiming to Please

Have you Out

Before the Referee start the Count

The Opponent don't stand a Chance

With his Hands Behind his Head

How are you going to get out of this?

She'll Knock you to your Knees

Once the Opponent is on the Floor

He'll be Bagging for Mercy

While he's Flat on his Back

With his Knees in the Air

Spread your Legs Wide Open

Let me in there

Dimples Licks her way on Top

Put her Hair in his Hand

Her Head going Back while the Opponent

Go Up Down Up Down Up Down

Dimples does this Amazing thing
When the Opponent thinks he got her
She Flips around while on Top Making her Opponent
Moan, Groan out loud

Making that Annoying sound
She Flips again put an Object in his Mouth
Make him Suck like a Baby
Until he gets enough it all comes out

The Grand Finale is when she get on her Fours
Need I say more
That Position took him out
He was in asleep hold for the Rest of the Night

Dimples stood over him like Smoker on Friday
YOU GOT KNOCKED THE F*** OUT!

WAKE UP! RISE UP

You think you going to Live Forever

You think this Country

Was a Created Equal Country

My Ignorance

Made me close my Ear to what is True

You don't know the Day that it maybe you

This Target is on Me wherever I go

My Skin, My Walk, My Talk

Is so Bold & Black

When I WAKE UP every day

I Pray to the Lord my Soul to Take

WAKE UP! RISE UP

You think you going to Live Forever

What do you think when get up every day?

This Country was Created for you to Fight

Who are we going to hear about tonight

WAKE UP! RISE UP

You think you going to Live Forever

Got a Call on April Fool

My Brothers both were found Dead

By their Own Color

While Waiting for them to say April Fools

This was Reality they were Gone

How about Making your Mind up today

Live like it's your Last Birthday

Stop the Violence they say

"It's your Own Hands that put you away"

WAKE UP! RISE UP

You think you're going to Live Forever

You think you're going to getting away

Nobody will know is what you say

You killing your Own Self when you think

That won't happen to me

This Target on my Back

You can see it in the Light

It's Brighter in the Dark

Don't Die WITHOUT Standing for Something

You will Live Standing for Nothing

As a Believer even I question God

This World is NOT my Home

One of these days I'll be Gone

Nobody can take a Life without Giving One

The Life you take will take yours One Day

You better Live Life like it's your Last Birthday

This Color Skin is Dying Fast

Don't even know how long I will Last

Let's start today by just doing
What's right even in the Dark
Only God can Judge your Heart

What are you doing?
If you got caught
Will it Destroy your Life?

Stop the Violence in your Own Mind
You won't get so Lucky the Next Time

Why are you Afraid to Try?
Some of you are setting here Dying with Purpose
How many know God Created you for a Reason?

You have the Ability to go as far as you can Dream
Why are you afraid to try
If the Bible say that God has given us power to get worth
Where are my Worthy people?

It's Frustrating to see

All the Opportunities around me

Who are you going to Blame today?

When God take the opportunities away

We talk about what we want to do

How about you Stop Making Excuses

For what's already prepared for you

Why are you afraid to try?

Don't be Jealous when your friends

Goes before you

God is the One to make your

Dreams Come True

I'm Waiting for that Day to come

When the Skies the Limit

My Destiny

LADIES!

LADIES!

They say if it Don't Kill You

It will make you Stronger

That we were built for this!

Well, I'm here to tell you

That Women too are Tired of being Tested

Mothers, Sistahs, Servants, Souljahs

Now is the Time for us to Rise

To Reclaim our Rightful Place!

Peace is where we Deserve to be

Because We are

Irresistible, Remarkable, Powerful, Unstoppable

Forever Holding Down our place in this World

A World that tries to Deny us our Freedom

BUT NO MORE

Not My Daughter!

You see,

Peace is what my Grandmother Prayed for

Justice is what my Mother Died for

A future for my Daughter is what I Fight for

So...

No Longer will we Sit Back on this Bus called Life

No Longer will we Quietly sit in Silence

Waiting for Change

No Longer will we be pushed

Into compromised positions

Because today is the Day our Souls Scream

Freedom and Equality!

HAVE YOU EVER BEEN IN A PLACE?

Where you just Don't Care?

Has your Tolerance Level ever been at

Because you are "Trapped" in a body that is

Uncontrollable!

Trapped in this,

This place and it got me Feeling all Crazy Inside

My Fantasies are so Unreal for a Christian Lady

Like me to Reveal, I should be Shame

But I'm not

Trapped by what society has labeled me!

Trapped but Freedom is where I crave to be

When I Open my Mouth, my Tongue is Unstoppable

I'm so Sick and Tired of being Stuck in this

Goody Goody Image

I wanna Release the Hood in me
Huh! I wanna be free
They want me to follow this Holy Path
And turn the other Cheek too

That's just too much for a real woman like me to do
My Life is such a Merry Go Round
It's always something Trying to keep me Down

If it's not the Kids, it's the Car Notes
Let's just face it, I need No Thrills, Less Bills
See this life is like that Crackerjack Box
With a Surprise on the Inside.

You just never know what you're going to get
I'm in this place that nothing surprises me anymore
But my Peace right now is Unbelievable
It's amazing how I'm just moving on through

Ladies

It's okay to be Selfish sometimes

Ain't nothing wrong with getting you

A Little Me Time

I done Gave all I'm gon' Give

Breath, Exhale, and just Freakin Live

Lula Ellis
CORONA!

Why do you take them out like this?

What is your Secret?

Mask on my Face, Gloves on my Hands

Sanitizer in my bag

CORONA!

You are not only a Cough, Fever, and Thief of lungs too.

You are a Virus that just don't care

No Color, No Ethnicity, No Economic Status

CORONA!

Do you have a list on people?

Are you marking them off as you go

Elderly, Diabetics, and Sickly

All of them are Vulnerable

CORONA!

You don't Play Fair

What's the use of me getting $1200.00

Not knowing Day to Day

When you're going to Stop

Lord have Mercy on our Soul!

Regretfully, Dimples

Lockdown for the Nation News

Filled with Body Bags

Families not able to have a decent burial

Unbelievable!

What I'm thinking?

Lying in my Bed with Tears in my Eyes

Looked up!

God what's happening?

My mind began to wonder

As my conversation with God got real

Just imagine God talking back,

"Daughter you have the chance to get it right."

Repent! Turn from your Wicked Ways
Make Me the Center of your Life Again

Fear became my Friend
Didn't know who to Trust
Listening to everybody's Revelation

God was trying to tell me something
What was going on inside of me Showed
Looking in the Mirror

Hate, Disappointment, Unforgiveness too
All became a Part of my Life
It's time to Purge!
Let is All Go

Thoughts after each Cough
CORONA got me Feeling Crazy up in here
Let me make sure everything is Clear
Debt Paid in Full before this Virus Kills me

Made a couple of Phone Calls

Moving through the week Preparing

Repent! Turn from your Wicked Ways

God began to Speak Again

Forgive me for Sin has taken Control

Falling to my Knees

Please Spare Me This Day

Oh Lord

Making it right with God is what I'm thinking

When Glorious that Day Comes

God! Please say well done

GROWING UP IN THE MISSISSIPPI DELTA

When I think about growing up in the Mississippi Delta with my brothers; my fondest memories stem from the times when mommy was alive. Those were some extremely beautiful times for our family. My brothers and I would come home from school each day and be met by the smell of homemade southern cooking. There were times when mom would walk to pick us up from the bus stop with her tall slender legs which were smoother than a shaved head. My mom would always have to get my older brother out of a fight with the neighborhood bullies. She didn't have her front teeth, so they would make fun of her as she would yell, "Let my boy go!" The bullies would laugh at her slur as she spoke. Mom would get my brother home, tie him to a chair as the belt would go up and down in her hands. Although she was a woman, she did her best to raise her sons.

Although neighborhood bullies existed during our childhood, the Delta Boys always found a way to come back together without causing bloodshed and extreme harm to any community. I did not have a many female friends, so I had to play with the Delta Boys. And even then, I learned that there was an unspoken unity and community love they all had for each other. Back then, we didn't see the types of violence our children are witnessing now. During those times, the neighborhood boys would all get together and play football, even after a fist fight. Sadly, today this is not the case. What happened? How do we get back to effective conflict and resolution practices?

As I sit in my lounge chair today reminiscing and sharing my thoughts of some amazing times living in the projects, it makes me realize how unique our childhood experiences were living in the Mississippi Delta. In our home, mommy would always have the Bible turned to book of Psalms 91. At the time I didn't know why or what it meant, but I knew it had to be important. I knew at an early age that there was something about the word of God that mommy depended on. I knew that the other mothers of the Delta Boys depended on it too. Maybe that was why the Delta Boys were able to agree to disagree without extreme violence and bloodshed. Maybe that's why we were all able to wake up each morning without living in fear of being murdered throughout the day. Maybe that's why the Delta Boys, although Black, were able to truly enjoy their elementary and high school years.

The moral to the story is that we should value having the word of God in our hearts. God's word should not only be important to us, but to our children. We need to minister the word of God to our sons and daughters. Mom made sure we knew that the Lord is most definitely our shepherd and we shall not want. The Lord is placing our men back into their rightful places. God had to allow an angel, Mr. George Floyd, to stand in the gap for the world's current transformation process. Black men get ready to make history again! Stand up and take your places! Do it with boldness! God has given you a second chance to shine. AMEN!

Romance, Power, & Religion in the Mind of a Godly Woman

BLACK LADY

BLACK LADY

The Twist is my Hair

Make people want to Stare

My Dark Chocolate Covered Face

Too Good to Waste

My Lips 👄 so Soft

To the Touch of the Man

BLACK LADY

Is who I was created to be

My reality hit when 2020 came

This Skin has a lot of Pain & Joy to this World

BLACK LADY IS ME

The way my Neck turns from Side to Side

My Big Hips and Thighs

The Loudness of my Voice

Power comes with the Right Connections

I AM A BLACK LADY

Education to the Community

A Slave to God's Purpose

NO LONGER will the System keep me Down

This BLACK LADY tastes the air of freedom

BLACK LADY IT'S ME

Lula Ellis
COLLEGE STUDENT ESSENTIAL WORKER

On my way to the Hospital

Wishing I could Stay in Bed

The story behind the Scenes

Tents set up for Overflow of Corona Patients

No Visitors to be Found

Too Quiet to be called a Hospital

The Corona Pandemic is Real

Patients having to Fight the Virus alone

This make you Appreciate Living

When patients are about to Die

The Nurses and Doctors carrying on like Normal

Make me think that it's become Insensitive

No more Feelings of Remorse

So many people Dying

My Prayer is to not Forget to Sympathize

Too Young to Die is what I'm thinking
Too Old to NOT care

By: Ishmael Kelly

YOUR WORDS ARE NOT THE TRUTH

Your Eyes exposed the Lack of Evidence

Just Tired of your Tied Lies

Your Ignorance was Unbelievable

You say that you Love Me

Your Actions were Unreal

Why make a Vow, you Coward

Chances just Increased the Delete

I'm Oblivious to your See-Through Heart

We Absorb Energy through time Spent

It's like being around a Sick Person

It's like having the Flu

It's that easy to Start Acting like You

Truth is Hard for you to tell

When you talk, I'm Aloof

Refuse to be Manipulated by a Man

Letting you know it's Not a Game

My Worth is MORE than what you offer

You Feening for Sex not the Queen

No woman can Replace the Original

I'm a Rare Jewel

I'm Valuable apparently Overpriced

They Fear to Lose, Break, or Damage it

Learn to Stop your Malicious ways

You might get Lucky again one day

By Chrysantheum Ellis

BLACK MEN

I know You are Angry

Frustrated

And Tired

Tired Of Wondering when will this cycle end?

For as long as we can remember

It's been a Badge and Abusive Authority

Our people have been Broken and Beaten

Till our souls submitted

BUT NO MORE!

Cause this is OUR time to make History

No Longer will a Generational Curse

Curse this Generation

No Longer will our Black Backs

Be Target Practice for Blue Scopes

Who see our Color as our Crime

And It doesn't matter your Titles, Status, or Hood

You have ALWAYS been seen as a Threat

Not as Fathers, Business Owners or Providers

Everything about you says that you are a Fighter

A Strong, Unstoppable, Unmovable

And forever changing Force of Nature

No more Knees or Nooses

That Loose us from our Families

No more Legislation that leads to Strangulation

So, without hesitation

Black

Man

Breathe

This time We can't Lose our Heads

This time We must be Lead...

By a Higher Power

So that the children see you

Stand up Straight

Raise your Chin

And Hold your Head High

Breathe

Breathe

I mean you Better Breathe

Cause Black Men

We can't breathe (Take a deep breath)

Without

You

TO BE NORMAL AGAIN

When asked how I feel about the Pandemic

I say It's Cool, I'm Fine, Not really!

I don't Miss School

But I do Miss the Freedom

I Miss hanging out in the Cafeteria

Eating three times a day

"No parents to answer too"

Access to the Dance Studio

Classes are now Online

It's not a Big Difference

Cause It's still like being in Class

But it is easier to Pass the Classes

Cause the Quizzes are Open Book

My dad has me in the House

He say he's afraid of me being Exposed

I'm not Scared

But I'm gon' stay Inside anyway

The Research in my English class
Taught me a lot about the Virus
My chances are Slim

I think people have Changed
Because of this Pandemic
This has Exposed a lot of Motives

It's also Exposed the Issues
We have in this World today
It's good for the Earth
That a lot of people are not out
It also Shows how busy the World really was

It Confused a lot of people
I'm used to Staying at Home anyway
But I just want things to be Normal again

By Chrysanthemum Ellis
Chrysanthemum is a Sophomore
At Savanah State University in Savanah Georgia

FIRE PURIFIES

You were Created to make things Hot
Most Valuable when placed Under Pressure
The Red Desire of a Burning Flame
Wish you were here to Melt away the Pain

Just thinking about you makes me Sweat
I need you to Remove the things that Don't Belong
Make me Clean with Passionate Warmth
Can't Imagine not being in the Fire with you

My Heart is a Flame
The Heat from your Heart
Changes the Shape of my Desire

Its Shine Brighter than Gold
Your Love Created something so Beautiful
With you I feel NO Cold
Only a warmth from deep within
Make me clean with your passionate flame
AND PURIFY ME WITH FIRE

MY BLACK SKIN

MY BLACK SKIN

MY BLACK SKIN
Is Known all over the World
My Bold look is known to Change the Lives
Of Boys and Girls

I'm a Produce of the Three Women
That Stood Out most to me
This is how my Vision of my Life will be

Come! Let me take you on a Journey in my Mind
You will Understand in Due Time
If I was to be a Bible Character
I'll choose Deborah

Deborah is one of the most influential women of the Bible. As a prophet, Judge Deborah was said to hear God's voice and share God's Word with others. As a priestess, she did not offer sacrifices, as the men did, but she did lead worship services and preach.

Deborah teaches me that you can be a leader but know how to submit as a wife. Deborah showed strength as a man but humility as a servant.

Who wouldn't want to be like Deborah?

If I was to be a Historian,
I'll choose Harriet

Harriet Tubman Born into slavery; Tubman escaped and subsequently made 13 missions to rescue approximately 70 enslaved people, including family and friends using the network of antislavery activists and safe houses known as the Underground Railroad. Wikipedia

This would be a Great Position for me
This is what my Mind See
Although Harriet faced Danger All Around
Harriet wasn't Afraid to Lay Her Life Down

As a Sacrifice you see
Harriet Sounds Like Me

Who wouldn't want to be like Harriet Tubman?

If I was to be a Celebrity
I'll choose Oprah Winfrey

Oprah Winfrey is a talk show host, media executive, actress and a billionaire. She's best known for being the host of her own, wildly popular program, The Oprah Winfrey Show, which aired for 25 seasons, from 1986 to 2011. In 2011, Winfrey launched her own TV network, the Oprah Winfrey Network (OWN).

Who wouldn't want to be like Oprah?

These Ladies stood out the Most to Me
After the Pain they Endeavored you see
The Glory of the Lord was Revealed in their Lives
These Stories remind Me of the times I had to Survive

Even though I Lived in the Projects

My Mind was in the Palace

I'm not a Product of what you see

I was created to be royalty

KINGS & QUEENS!

They say if it DON'T Kill us,

It will Make us Stronger

That we were Built for this!

Well,

I'm here to tell you that

We both Men & Women are Tired of being Tested

Mothers, Sistahs, Servants, Souljahs

Now is the time for us to Rise

To Reclaim Our Rightful Place!

Peace is where we Deserve to be

Because WE are

Irresistible

Remarkable

Powerful

Unstoppable

Forever holding down our Place in this World

A world that Tries to Deny us our Freedom
BUT NO MORE!
Not My Son or Daughters You see

Peace is what my grandmother prayed for
Justice is what my mother died for
A future for my children is what I fight for

So...
No longer will we sit back on this bus called life
No longer will we quietly sit in silence waiting for change
No longer will we be pushed into compromised positions

Because today is the Day our Souls Scream
Freedom and Equality!
Today is a time to Remember

Never forget that in each of us is a Life Force
That will move Mountains if we STAND TOGETHER!
So, Let not your Hearts be Troubled No Longer Stand!

WE WILL WIN

Head up, Back Straight & Move

This System will NO LONGER Break Us

It will make us...More Unified than ever

We will Push our way Through this

This will not be just another Gathering

Change has Taken Place already today

We have made History

We are going to Continue to Fight

We will not get Tired &

WE WILL WIN

We just let the Songs Play

As We Lay started us off

While Moving to the Bedroom

We Forgot About Tomorrow

No time to Wait moving that Black Silk Sasha

Over My Head

Purple Rain all over the Room

As the Lights were Clapped off

Clap! Clap! Clap!

My Body All Over Your Body

Feel the Fire coming from my Enter

Though the Heat as my Legs Move

Slow it Down as he kissed my Neck

Move to my Side Down to my Toe

Need I give more?

You're Making me High

Off just the Touch of your Hands

The Heat off your Tongue

The Vibration of your Man

I'm thinking How Deep is Your Love

He started Singing to Me

I Wanna Tease You, I Wanna Please you

I wanna Show you Baby, That I Need You

I Want Your Body, 'Till the Very Last Drop

I Want You to Holler When You Want Me to Stop...

Who Can Love Like Me "NOBODY"

Things were getting Out of Hand

As he Turned me on my Belly

The Smoke from his Nostrils

Made the Hair on my Back Stand

I started Shaking with Intense Motion

Anticipating the Next Move

He went Down and Back Up

My Toes Start Popping

We made So Much Noise

Waking up EVERYBODY in the House

I Didn't See Nothing Wrong

With a Little Bump-N- Grind

ABOUT THE AUTHOR

Lula Ellis was born in Greenwood, MS to the late Genette Carr, but currently resides in Fort Worth, TX. Lula received her BA in Sociology from M.V.S.U. on May 9, 1998 and MA in Professional Development from D.B.U. on December 19, 2008.

Lula has been blessed with two wonderful children Chrysantheum Ellis and Ishmael Kelly. Lula is the CEO/Founder of Lend Me Your Ear Ministries which is a non-profit organization for needy families. Lula Ellis is a radio show personality, poet, minister, event coordinator, and emcee.

She is one of the most charismatic people on the planet. Her trademark laugh will have you feeling warm and welcomed.

www.ingramcontent.com/pod-product-compliance
Lightning Source LLC
Chambersburg PA
CBHW070914080526
44589CB00013B/1289